lighting

lighting
recipes and ideas

Sally Storey

QUADRILLE

First published in 2000 by
Quadrille Publishing Limited,
Alhambra House,
27–31 Charing Cross Road,
London WC2H 0LS

This paperback edition first published in 2003

Editorial Director: Jane O'Shea
Consultant Art Director: Helen Lewis
Project Editor: Nicki Marshall
Design Assistant: Sarah Emery
Production: Julie Hadingham
Special Photography: Tom Stewart
Picture Researcher: Nadine Bazar

British Library Cataloguing-in-Publication Data
A catalogue record for this book is available
from the British library.

ISBN 1 84400 045 1

Printed and bound in Singapore.

To Lucca, Cazalla and Alexander

Page 1: Decorative patterns created by a traditional lantern.

Page 2: Wall-mounted uplights provide the general light in the room.
The wire track system has pendant spotlights over the table
and small, directional spotlights at either end. The wires
carry the current and are powered by a remote transformer.

Page 5: A narrow-beam spotlight provides a central focus
to the dining table, reflecting light over the place
settings.

Publisher's note
Throughout the book measurements are given in both metric
and imperial. When planning any lighting scheme or when buying
fixtures follow either all metric or all imperial measurements, as the
two are not necessarily interchangeable.

contents

1

introduction

Lighting is one of the most difficult design concepts to understand. Light is all around us but we cannot touch or feel it, and yet it is responsible for all that we see; without light we perceive nothing. Interior designers use colour swatches or samples to demonstrate a creative effect and to help make decisions, but it is difficult to prepare a sample board of 'lighting effects'. The way light is used will, in fact, change the way that we see everything.

The potential of light has long been exploited in the theatre, where the powerful combinations of light and shade, tone and colour are used to create the mood for each set and direct our focus towards important characters or objects around the stage. The same detailed understanding of lighting is fundamental to photography. There is no reason why domestic lighting should not create the same powerful effects as in artistic disciplines.

Light and shade

Good lighting stems from an understanding of the balance between light and shade. In simple terms, lighting is the presentation of space. If used skilfully, it provides the final invisible touches to your design. Artificial light thrown onto the surfaces of a room from different heights and angles will change its apparent dimensions. It can emphasize height, structure and materials, and become almost an architectural element itself.

Whether your interior is traditional or contemporary, the lighting will set the mood. But good lighting should not really be noticed: it should enhance your interiors and provide a wonderfully creative environment without *obviously* doing so. To the unpractised eye, it is only bad lighting that is noticed. This may be because it is too bright or too dark, because the light sources glare into your eyes or because it draws attention to the wrong elements of a room.

For many people, the traditional central pendant is their main source of light – lighting in all directions but with little focus or direction. This type of lighting is unexciting and rarely fulfils a room's potential; combined with table lamps and other light sources, however, it can be effective.

1 This halo effect is created by a floating canvas panel surrounded by fluorescent tubes with blue filters to colour the light.

2 The play of sunlight, shining through the grid at an angle, creates wonderful speckled patterns of light across the wall.

3 Natural light filters through slatted blinds, and combines with the warmth of a table lamp for a soft, daytime scheme.

The creative potential of modern lighting is discussed here, along with how to use its flexibility to best effect. Light can be manipulated to dim, brighten, obscure and highlight, and to create plays of shadow and colour; it can transform the atmosphere of a room just as theatrical lighting transforms a scene. This is the great advantage of lighting over all other design aspects. Good lighting design means flexibility; it enables a family kitchen used for the preparation of food, for example, to be changed at the flick of a switch from a bright, functional space into an intimate dining area for a party.

Lighting techniques

It is important to understand from the beginning that good lighting is usually made up of a number of effects. Just as an interior decorator layers textures and paint finishes, a lighting designer will use a variety of different lighting techniques in each room to achieve an overall result. It is by balancing the intensity of the various effects that lighting moods are created.

This book gives an introduction to the use of this evocative element of decoration. First, it gives a description of the basic tools and techniques. It then goes through a

house room by room considering the lighting requirements of each, as well as any special problems they may pose. None of the suggested ideas is, however, the only solution, as interior lighting offers endless potential and variety. The suggestions are for inspiration and to demonstrate a palette of lighting effects so that you can decorate with light just as an artist uses colour. With this in mind, it is essential to understand some of the powerful tools available to the lighting designer. These can be summarized as the light source itself, and the method of how the light is manipulated within a room or garden.

1 Surrounded by open space and woodland, this house has little need for privacy and so natural light can flood in. On winter evenings, candles along the window ledge and a log fire add softness and warmth, but the outside view is the focus.

2 If a garden feature, such as a tree or fountain, is lit from the outside, a focus is produced beyond the glass to create a feeling of spaciousness. This helps to eliminate the problem of a window appearing like a mirror after dark.

3 A blue neon tube has been recessed into the ceiling to cast light down this frosted glass wall.

1 Recessed low-voltage uplights, close to the wall, create narrow shafts of light up the wall and reflected light from the ceiling. Downlights recessed into the ceiling provide both downward light and a wall wash effect, due to their proximity to the wall.

2 This soft tungsten uplight effect can be achieved either with clickstrip or architectural tubes to provide definition around the ceiling. The warmth of the tungsten contrasts with the bright whiteness of the cupboards.

There are six main lighting tools: downlighting, uplighting, wall washing, feature lighting, colour and control. These fall within the overall divisions of general lighting, task lighting and feature lighting.

Uplighting, downlighting and wall washing can be used to create the general lighting if several light sources are positioned around the room. Used individually, they can provide feature lighting by creating a focus on flowers or a painting, for example, or even highlighting an architectural feature. Similarly, when used individually they can provide useful task lights, such as those needed for reading or cooking. The elements of feature and task lighting overlay the general lighting to create an effective scheme for each room.

Downlighting

Of the modern approaches to lighting, downlighting is possibly the most conventional. It is direct and generally energy-efficient, as it concentrates the lighting in the specific area where it is required. Downlights, usually recessed into the ceiling, form a three-dimensional cone, or arc, of light which will vary in size depending on the beam angle. If you concentrate downlights within the centre of a room the cone of light will not spill onto the wall and create unwanted 'arcs' of light.

Downlighting is often used imaginatively, but excessive use of it in this way can make a room appear gloomy, as the floor is well-lit whilst the walls and ceiling remain in shadow. In these instances, some light on the walls may be desired. This is why it is important to understand lighting design in three dimensions and the effect of an arc of light across a wall. You should position your downlights not so as to create a symmetrical pattern of light on the ceiling, but to achieve the best effects on your walls: the closeness of your downlight to the wall and the beam width of your bulb (see page 98) will affect the pattern of light on the wall. A downlight with a wide beam when positioned close to a wall will make the arc of light begin higher. Downlighting tends to work best in rooms with high ceilings as the beams of light created overlap, and the light becomes more diffuse.

Uplighting

Uplighting enhances a sense of height, making a room appear more spacious than it is. The principal purpose of uplights is to direct light up at the ceiling, which acts as a reflector. If your ceiling is light in colour, this will provide a very diffuse, general light whilst creating a sense of space. Uplights offer more flexibility than downlights: they can be wall-mounted or free-standing, high- or low-level and are available with a wide number of different bulb (lamp) types.

Ideally, uplights should be positioned in pairs to give a sense of symmetry. Due to the intensity of their light, halogen uplights at the side of a room can create sharp lines across the wall, so you must ensure that this line does not cut across a picture or piece of furniture. If the lights are positioned in front of a window or mirror this line of light will not be noticed, and against a dark wall the beam shape could become a feature in itself. Tall, free-standing uplights come in many different styles to suit every interior. If using these, it is worth plugging them into a 5-amp outlet so that they can be dimmed when required (see page 90). A floor-standing, drum-shaped uplight can be used with a low-voltage bulb as an excellent way of lighting dark corners of a room.

Wall washing

These are ceiling-mounted fixtures which direct their light evenly across a wall and can provide part of the general lighting. Unlike downlights and uplights, wall washers emphasize the vertical surfaces in your room, and are especially useful in enlarging the perceived width of a room. As with other techniques, the brighter the colour of the wall, the greater amount of reflected light.

Wall washers are also useful when emphasizing wall texture, pictures or cupboards. Similar in appearance to downlights, they will need either to be adjustable or have an additional reflector (see page 98) to direct the light. The positioning of wall washers is critical to ensure an even distribution of light. For best effect, fittings usually need to be 700–1000mm (28–40in) apart, and distance from the wall depends on the type of fixture and the ceiling height.

Feature lighting

Feature lighting

This can be used to highlight chosen features in a room, whilst hiding less significant details. Feature lighting works best when the light source itself remains hidden: your eye is naturally drawn to the brightest point within a room, and if the bulb or fitting were visible this would be the focus. A recessed fitting which spotlights a picture or a narrow-beam uplight which highlights a column or arch work well. Low-voltage, miniature directional sources are the most versatile solution. You need to pay special attention to the position of the fittings and use the right beam width for the object being lit. To highlight a wall-mounted feature, the light should be positioned between the viewer and the wall.

You need to create the right intensity of light to make the most of each object, and not bleed out any colour by overlighting or bleaching it. It is recommended that the feature lighting within a room is controlled separately from the general lighting to maximize the effect (see page 90).

Colour

Rather than coloured filters or lamp as in photography, 'colour' for the lighting designer is the selection of a light source to emphasize the true colour of what is being lit. Different light sources have different colour temperatures. For example, a standard GLS (tungsten) bulb, a fluorescent and a low-voltage halogen bulb (see pages 92–7) each give out a very different light that is dependent on the colour temperature. The easily-recognizable tungsten bulb has a soft, yellow light which is warm and inviting at night, but can seem dull in the daytime. The crisp whiteness of halogen light, on the other hand, is far better when used in dark areas during the day as it is more compatible with daylight. At night, though, it can seem cool, but when dimmed will achieve the same warmth as the standard GLS source.

A fluorescent source can be either cool or warm in colour depending on the fixture selected. When buying lights, look for the particular code written on the packaging which gives the colour temperature. Different light sources can be combined within a scheme if they are controlled separately.

The fitting's reflector (see page 98) also affects the colour. For example, a gold reflector will give a warm quality to the light, whilst a silver reflector gives a slightly cooler light. Reflectors within some table lamp shades can also be gold or silver, and have a similar effect on the light.

Control

'Control' is the term lighting designers use for fine-tuning lighting to achieve maximum flexibility and ease of use: the more control a scheme has, the more flexible it is. It is highly recommended to separate the general lighting from both the feature lighting and task lighting. If only a single dimmer was used in each room for all lights, then they would be dimmed together and the relative brightness between the various light sources would remain the same. Control balances the lighting effects to create different atmospheres: at its most simple this is 'on' or 'off', bright or dim. However, a more complicated pre-set system (see page 90) can balance all the

switchlines (see page 98) to exactly the right level and memorize them so that, at the touch of a button, a different mood is instantly achieved. The advantage here is that you do not need to dim each switchline individually.

It is best to try to keep your light effects separate. If, for example, downlights and a lantern are providing general light in a hall, they should be controlled individually and separately, because their light sources are different.

1 Recessed narrow-beam, low-voltage uplights highlight the flowers, whilst low-voltage lights skim out across each step creating a dramatic play of light and shadow.

2 The low-voltage downlights, with frosted lenses, give a gentle, scalloped effect on the cupboards, and the narrow beam downlights create a shaft of light on the stainless steel. There are also four downlights in the centre, providing a soft, general light on the floor.

The lighting from the galley above spills onto the kitchen. A narrow, downward focus of light on the table gives a sense of intimacy. Low-voltage down- and uplights give an unusual working light to the kitchen counter.

Layering of light creates different focuses in this large studio. Spotlights provide pools of light on the artwork and library shelves, while local reading lights offer task lighting by the chairs. Care should be used when positioning spotlights, so that their light is not thrown too far or creating unwanted glare.

Light sources

These days, there are endless varieties of light sources. The main sources used within the home are tungsten filament, tungsten halogen, both mains- and low-voltage, and compact fluorescent. Others, such as discharge sources, metal halide and sodium (see page 98), have a delayed start up and are not easy to dim. For this reason they are used mainly in commercial situations, although they are sometimes useful in gardens to light up large trees and to provide the light source for fibre optics.

Tungsten filament (or incandescent)

This is the standard bulb in most table lamps we use and is available in a variety of shapes and sizes (see page 92). Electricity passes along the tungsten filament (see page 98), heating it so that a mixture of light and heat is produced. The resulting light is warm and inviting, which is effective in the evening, but can look unnatural and insipid during the day. For best results, this type of light source should be combined with others so that a different balance is achieved between light levels for daytime and evening.

Tungsten halogen

This bulb contains a tungsten filament as before, but is surrounded by a halogen gas. The halogen combines with the tungsten to provide a far whiter and brighter light than the equivalent tungsten. It is often used for uplighting.

The tungsten halogen linear fixtures (200–300 watts), whether wall-mounted or free-standing, can be the perfect solution to the general light for a room with an ornate or sloped ceiling or unusual shape. The conventional tungsten halogen lamps work very well as uplights, giving a white light and, with their high wattage, a correspondingly high level of illumination.

Tungsten filament bulbs can be used in bowl uplights to give a warmer, softer light than tungsten halogen. Where a high level of light is required, perhaps in a child's bedroom, family room, kitchen or work area, the whiter light of the tungsten halogen source may be more appropriate.

Low voltage tungsten halogen

Low voltage means that a bulb fitting operates at 12 volts (v) rather than the usual 240v. The advantage of 12v is that the filament in the lamp can be manufactured much smaller, which results in a more discreet light source which can still control the light efficiently. The spread of light is determined by the position of the filament within the reflector; if the filament is in the wrong place, dark spots can appear in the light beam.

Low-voltage bulbs particularly lend themselves to feature lighting: they enable very precise control and provide an attractive white light because of their halogen gas. To reduce the voltage from 240v to 12v a transformer is required (see page 98). If an electronic transformer is used with downlights, it can usually fit through the aperture of the fitting and rest in the ceiling alongside the fitting. If maintenance is required, the transformer can be pulled out of the ceiling through the hole of the fixture itself.

Fluorescent

Unlike the filament of a tungsten lamp heating up, this consists of a glass tube coated with a fluorescent phosphor powder and containing an inert low-pressure gas such as argon. When electricity is passed through the tube the phosphorous layer is activated and emits light. Although four times more efficient than a tungsten source, the light quality is flatter and less focused so is not normally used for feature lighting. It is often used as a task light under kitchen cabinets or as a general light source in a garage, but can also be used as an uplight above cupboards or shelves.

Smaller compact fluorescent sources can be used in downlights and, as long as they have special control equipment, such as a high-frequency dimmable ballast (see page 98), they can be dimmed. The start up voltage required is provided by the ballast. When a tungsten filament is dimmed, less light is produced and the light becomes warmer in character; when a fluorescent is dimmed, the light source will also produce less light, but the colour temperature of the source does not change as the eye expects and so sometimes produces a somewhat 'grey', dull effect.

Fibre optics

The use of fibre optics is becoming more widespread. In essence, this source uses a remote light box (see page 98). Light is focused at one end of a bunch of individual glass fibres, and is then transmitted down the fibres to emit at the other end. This light is particularly suitable for the display of sensitive items because no heat or ultraviolet (UV) is emitted. It is also useful for providing light in places where access is problematic, as the light source is remote and, therefore, easier to maintain. The light source can be either metal halide or tungsten halogen, depending on the power required.

Before you start

Before starting to plan the lighting for each room, look at the space to be lit. What are its best points? What atmosphere will be most appropriate? Identify the furniture plan within the room and where pictures and other important items will be positioned. Identify the colour scheme and finishes so that you know what will be reflective and what will not. Identify the key features in a room, i.e. the main accent points – are there niches, shelves, ornaments or flowers on a table? What activities are to be performed in the room – reading, food preparation, etc.? Will special lighting be required? Does it need to be bright or will a special task light be required? When you have addressed all of these issues, you are ready to begin designing your lighting scheme.

1. Tungsten filament is the standard bulb used in most decorative table lamps and wall lights, and provides a soft, warm light.

2. Tungsten striplight has the same soft light as a tungsten bulb, with a similar characteristic warmth, but the filament is long and surrounded by a glass tube. It resembles the fluorescent in shape, but its lamp life is far shorter and light warmer.

3. Fibre optics provide a pattern of miniature stars on the ceiling. These are, in fact, created by a single light source, located remotely, which emits electricity down individual glass fibres in black sheaths which emit light at their ends.

2

recipes and ideas

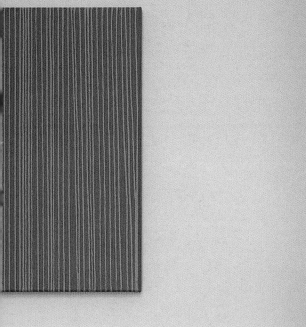

Designing lighting around the front door is vital since it is the first introduction to your house. Lighting schemes can be designed to make an impact on the street or be very discreet. At the entrance to your home, when the front door opens, hall lighting can be used to set the scene and create a wonderful impression by being both inviting and dramatic. Even in small spaces this is easy to achieve with planning.

entrances

As entrance halls are often small, narrow spaces with little room for furniture they require specific lighting solutions. The main objective when lighting a hall is therefore to create a bright, crisp effect, combining daylight and artificial light, to eliminate gloom. A common problem in narrow entrance halls is a shortage of natural light. If the hall is overlooked by a half-landing, a window at this position offers extra natural light and can act as a visual draw or focus to suggest space. This can also be achieved with artificial light at night.

1 The low-voltage downlights in this hall provide strong pools of light down the corridor and at the threshold of the next room. This contrasts with the uplight over the curved doorway which creates the general light in the reception room.

2 This entrance is lit using a standard tungsten lamp in a lantern, which provides an all-over general light, and lights a person at the door whilst creating an attractive visual focus.

Low-voltage downlights can be used to mimic daylight, but on their own will make the ceiling seem lower and the space smaller, as the light falls solely on the floor. Uplighting emphasizes the ceiling and provides a feeling of spaciousness. The best solution is to layer the light by combining uplighting and downlighting or, perhaps, a decorative pendant with downlights. If you use a variety of light effects which can be switched on at will or controlled separately, the mood in the hall can be altered throughout the day. Wall-mounted fittings do not often work in such a narrow space; uplights and downlights recessed into the walls, ceiling or floor are therefore an excellent alternative.

A central pendant can be retained if in keeping with the style of the room but, used alone, will provide a sharp, unattractive light. Supplement this with a pair of low-voltage downlights on either side to create a clean, daylight feel. Focus the downlights onto objects on the walls to provide a general wash.

Long corridors with no natural daylight require special attention. Various lighting elements can be used to create changing effects or highlight attractive features. For example, in a long, arched corridor a recessed cove light could provide a soft, continuous wash of light on one side of the room, whilst recessed low-glare uplights could be used close to the opposite wall to emphasize the arch.

① Downlights in a small space need not be centred; located close to one wall they create greater emphasis and a wall-wash effect.

An alternative way of making an entrance hall less gloomy is to create a focus in the middle distance. If a picture or object is lit on a half-landing, the eye will be drawn directly to this feature, distracting attention from the relative narrowness of the hall.

When lighting a very large hall, it is particularly important to create layers of lighting effects which you can alter during the day, since this may often be used as another reception room or work space. You may wish to use a central decorative fitting; if so, another layer of light should be added. If you have a table below your central fitting, this layering could be achieved by adding a number of low-voltage downlights around the central pendant to focus on the table, where flowers or a selection of books could be positioned.

The perimeter of the hall will require attention. Pictures could be highlighted, and a softness can be added to your lighting design by placing a lamp on a side table. Each of these effects, just as with any other room, would benefit from being controlled individually.

1 A spotlight, mounted on the wall above, lights the stair treads and a downlight at the top of the stairs draws your eye upwards. Two sculptured lamps provide the soft, general light and an interesting visual focus.

2 A small low-voltage downlight is recessed into each of the niches, which also produces a dramatic lighting effect on the objects. By lighting the niches, enough light is also thrown onto the stairs.

3 This unusual collection of chandeliers provide an interesting sparkle effect; they can be dimmed to give a soft, candle-light glow. They contrast with the rustic brick chimney, which is covered with candles and lit with tungsten wall washers to offer a reflected light over the stairs.

Lighting the landing

Lighting a half-landing is a good way
of also lighting stairs. Your eye is
always drawn to the brightest point,
here the half-landing, so you will
be almost led up to the top of the
stairs. The reflected light from the
light sources on the half-landing
also provide sufficient light for the
stairs themselves.

Floor wash lights

Floor wash lights, recessed into the
wall, offer light over individual stair
treads. A fitting with a wider wash
could be located over every third or
fourth tread. This technique is particularly useful when lighting basement
stairs, where there are often limited
locations for fittings and the sloping
ceiling of stairs above prevents the
use of downlights.

Individual stair lights

Recessed lights located in the stair tread above will light the steps individually. This technique, using a small low-voltage light source, throws light across the step or floor, and can be used to accentuate a change of level within a room.

Narrow stairs

Here the soft uplights are recessed into every fourth or fifth step to provide a wash over one of the side walls. It is a dramatic statement that, in this instance, is used to emphasize the narrowness of the space. Again, a brighter light creates focus at the top of the stairs.

ways to light a front door

Downlights

For a contemporary look, recessed downlights throw light onto the front door and create a pool of light on the top step. Use a low-voltage baffled (see page 98) downlight with a wide-beam bulb, located as close to the front door as possible: this will achieve a high arc of light on the door itself whilst reducing any shadow on a visitor's face. Teaming a well-lit front door with a warm and welcoming entrance hall is the perfect way to use lighting to invite guests to enter your home and walk through to the living area.

Up/downlights

Traditional wall lights could be replaced by something more original, such as a pair of up/downlights. These provide a strong architectural effect with their simultaneous lighting upwards and downwards. Used either side of the door, particularly in a porch, these fittings create a whole wash of bright light which makes a dramatic statement on the street and offers a vibrant welcome to guests. If you place a plant either side of the front door, they will be put into dramatic silhouette by these fittings.

Traditional lantern

An effective welcome is to position a tungsten hanging lantern over the porch or to locate a pair of decorative lantern-style wall lights either side of the entrance. These will provide a generous light on the threshold and will ensure that your guests are well-lit on arrival. If guests need to walk through a garden to the door, locate further lanterns on an adjacent wall, or, more dramatically, use spiked uplights (see page 98) under plants and pathlights (see page 98) to light the way.

Whatever the style of your living or dining room, whether traditional or contemporary, the lighting should be an integral part of the design, and should offer discreet solutions which are flexible enough for every activity. In a dining room the light should be bright, fresh and appealing at lunchtime, and soft and subdued at night, allowing enough light on the table whilst avoiding harsh shadows on diners' faces.

living spaces

In rooms which are in regular use throughout the day and evening, the lighting must adapt to suit different moods or functions. Successful lighting depends on the general, feature and task lighting working in harmony, in the same way that fabric colours and textures are chosen as part of the interior design. The solution you choose will depend on your style of decoration. By varying the levels of these individual effects, and by using different combinations, you can create both dramatic impact and the perfect light setting for every activity.

1 Rectangular slots in the ceiling are lit with a tungsten source and the reflected light gives in-fill ambient lighting. The pendant in the double-height space provides enough light for the large area and creates a visual focus.

2 The same space by day: natural light floods in and the slots in the ceiling remain in shadow, although the unlit pendant still offers an interesting focus.

Although a single, central pendant may complement the style of the room, the light it produces will be flat and dull. Used as a decorative feature, however, they do have their place as a focal point in the centre of a room. To provide general lighting, they can be supplemented with further sources of light around the room, such as an arrangement of table lamps or wall lights.

Table lamps can be positioned anywhere within a room: to eliminate darkness around the edges; reduce areas of shadow in the centre; or act as task lights for reading when located next to chairs and sofas, which will introduce a second layer of light. It is advisable to install floor sockets in the centre of the room to give yourself more flexibility in choosing where to place lamps, and also to eliminate the problem of cables trailing from sockets at the edge of the room to your lamp. Although they are an easy option for a living room, using too many lamps may give your home the appearance of a lamp shop, and so you should combine these with other light sources.

In contemporary settings, the general lighting is often achieved through methods other than pendants and table lamps. Downlighting, from fixtures installed in the ceiling or underneath cupboards, can effectively create a good overall light. If you choose this technique as part of your lighting scheme, mains-voltage fittings could be used, but they are somewhat bulky and so it may be better to opt for the low-glare, low-voltage alternative. Another advantage of low-voltage downlights is their crisp, white light. On a gloomy day, their brilliant light makes it seem as if the sun is literally shining in, making them particularly useful in rooms that receive little natural light.

Downlights are also very useful for adding light into the centre of a room, an area which can sometimes be forgotten; they can be directed onto a decorative object to work as both general and feature lighting. Downlights placed directly over seating areas create effective reading lights, but can cast distorted shadows of light across you when seated. If this task light is required, it would be useful to have the option of dimming the light to create a softer effect when entertaining.

A table lamp glows in the corner of the room, and candles work with flames from the fire to set the right mood.

A low-voltage uplight is concealed behind the chair to light the sculpture and balance the effect of the lamp.

Large lamps positioned beside the sofa provide both general and task lighting.

The picture light offers additional feature lighting and adds a highlight to the room.

Framing pictures with light

When lighting a picture you need to consider where on the wall it is being hung, how to bring out the best colour rendition and the type of frame it has. For instance, is the frame relatively flat and unobtrusive or large and deep? If the latter, you should beware the frame casting ugly shadows over the picture. And if the picture has a heavy glaze or glass frame, the wrong kind of lighting will produce unwanted reflections. You need to consider where in the picture is the detail and whether an even wash of light or a specific focus would be more dramatic.

One of the most effective, but expensive, forms of picture lighting is precisely to frame your picture with light. This involves projecting a light beam to the exact dimensions of the picture, which makes the picture appear as if it is internally illuminated. The picture is lit within the frame, leaving the frame itself unlit. It is a startling technique which accentuates the impact of the picture. It can be achieved with a number of spotlights and a few recessed fixtures which use various lenses and shuttering devices to achieve the required result. Considerable care needs to be taken in their positioning to achieve the correct beam coverage and ensure that they are lined up exactly with the picture so that the shuttering devices (see page 98) can be used effectively to focus the beam of light.

ways to light a picture

Free-standing spotlight

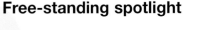

The crisp, white light of low-voltage halogen helps to bring out a picture's true colours. If a picture with a glass cover is lit, unwanted reflections may occur. Here, a spotlight is used as an uplight, which means that reflections are not visible as they are reflected towards the ceiling. With a spotlight, you need to use the appropriate beam width for your picture; a narrow beam is suitable for small artworks.

Frame-mounted light

With a picture light mounted on the frame, the picture should be effectively covered. An important consideration is the proximity of the light to the picture itself. If it is too close, the spread of light will only cover the top part of the picture. Additional light can be added, for example from a table lamp located below. Avoid using wall-mounted picture lights as they are more likely to light the wall instead.

Directional downlight

A recessed, low-voltage directional downlight can be an effective picture light when baffled to prevent glare. You need to decide on the hanging height of the picture (usually eye level), to calculate the most effective beam width and the exact distance from the wall that the fitting will be recessed into the ceiling. For larger pictures two light sources may be necessary.

Uplighting is a good solution for contemporary interiors as most uplights are of a modern design. Low-level, drum-shaped uplights (see page 98), either mains- or low-voltage, can be hidden behind a piece of furniture to light the corners of a room, or provide lighting in a bay window which appears dark at night. When positioned under plants, these uplights provide an interesting pattern of light on the walls and ceiling and will contribute to both the general and feature lighting. A free-standing halogen uplight will provide a high intensity of light in rooms when required.

Wall washing can be used to softly illuminate plain walls as an addition to general lighting, or to highlight a favourite piece of art. Both effects can easily be achieved in your living or dining room by using an array of downlights positioned in the ceiling between 50–100cm (20–40in) away from a wall, depending on ceiling height, and 1m (40in) apart. This works best if wide beam bulbs are used, possibly with a frosted cover lens (see page 98). The brightness of this light may overshadow more subtle effects if it is not balanced by other areas of light on the opposite side of the room.

Having set the scene with the general and task lighting, drama and contrast can be introduced through feature lighting. Some of the choices you will have made for your overall lighting scheme may offer some feature lighting, but additional effects will add focus to chosen objects or specific areas of the room. Flowers on a coffee or dining table can, for instance, be illuminated with a narrow beam of light, which will bring out the best in the flowers and create a central focal point in the room, making it appear more intimate.

1 A soft, low voltage tungsten striplight, concealed by low benches, provides a gentle uplight. Maximum reflection is achieved with plain, white walls.

2 In this instance a light fixture becomes art itself and adds an extra dimension to the lighting within the room.

3 General light is provided by the wall lights, and low-voltage recessed lights are positioned to highlight the picture and the flowers on the coffee table as additional feature lighting. Lighting the centre of rooms is important and often forgotten.

Drama can be created by highlighting the architectural features of a room, possibly a large open fireplace or an arched doorway. In a room with columns, you can achieve stunning effects with lights recessed into the floor and positioned close to the column bases, as the light will graze up the side and produce a dramatic focus at the top.

The illumination of an alcove, shelves or cabinet can be another form of focus and feature in a room. The simplest method of lighting shelves is to use a tungsten striplight behind a baffle (see page 98) which conceals the source. There are, however, two disadvantages with this method: the bulky size of the fitting requires large shelf sizes to conceal the source, and the linear filament is delicate and frequently 'blows'. An alternative solution is to use candle bulbs, and although several individual bulbs are required, they are cheaper than a single tungsten strip and last much longer. Low-voltage shelf-lighting systems, however, usually achieve the best results. They are smaller than the linear filament bulbs and therefore can be concealed within slimmer shelves. They normally consist of a small track system, or clickstrip (see page 97), so that bulbs can either be arranged uniformly along the length of a shelf or in clusters to light specific objects. They do require a remote transformer (see page 98) and can get quite hot, so they should not be used near books. To light a bookshelf effectively, a simple mains-voltage rope-light (see page 97) can be used, as it offers a soft light, is fairly small, has a long lamp life and does not get too hot.

Three-dimensional objects, like pieces of sculpture, offer the greatest canvas for dramatic lighting schemes. When lighting any object, the most important factors are the direction of light and the play between light and shadow, as distortions can result if the proportions and placing are not right. You also need to take into account the position from which the object will be viewed. Depending on the shape of the sculpture or ornament, and features within it that you wish to highlight, you can choose whether it should be uplit, downlit or backlit. If you want to install your lighting before the piece to be lit has been chosen, cross lighting (see page 98) will be the safest option, as it allows you to throw light from both sides.

1 This pendant is a strong visual focus: it softly accentuates the table and the shade will help provide a soft, diffuse light on diners' faces. The perimeter walls have strong feature lighting from recessed low-voltage sources.

2 Backlighting with a coloured filter on the frosted glass shelves provides a wash of atmospheric light to render the books in silhouette. The light becomes a theatrical backdrop here rather than functionally lighting the books.

Combination of designs

Two lighting designs create subtly different effects. Downlighting through glass shelves creates interesting shadows, while the sidelighting in the central section of the cabinet gives a uniform warm glow. This combination lights the shelves but leaves the structure of the cabinet in shadow.

Concealed light

Uplighting the cabinet itself creates further dramatic interest, highlighting the pilasters and creating pools of light over the architrave at the top. This is also a very successful way of providing indirect light in a room from a virtually concealed source.

creative
lighting for
display
cabinets

Downlighting

This miniature low-voltage downlight has a small baffle to reduce glare and is particularly good for bringing out the sparkle of glass objects. A 20w 12v, narrow-beam, dichroic MR11 lamp (see page 98) is powerful enough to punch light through the decanter and glass shelf to highlight the objects below. The decanter has been positioned to allow light to pass through to the shelves below.

Mini track system

A low-voltage shelf track system is concealed by the side profiles of the cabinet. The fitting can use either 3w, 5w or 8.5w 12v festoon lamps (see page 98), at 50mm (2in) intervals; if a larger gap were left, other areas of light and shade would be created. The effect here is a soft, even glow suitable for lighting most objects, whether ceramics, earthenware or glass.

Uplighting

Recessed low-voltage uplights set into the base of the unit employ 20w 12v, narrow-beam, metal reflector lamps (see page 98), fitted with a glare cap to reduce the direct view of the light source. Light grazes the outside of the cabinet, while the objects themselves are lit by downlights flooding through the shelves above.

Defining a route

Downlights emphasize the corridor route to the central dining area within this house. As the table remains unlit it is not the natural focus within the room. For dining an alternative lighting scheme is required.

Filtered daylight

The venetian blinds allow a diffused light to wash over the dining table throughout the day, which is perfect for reading, working, relaxing or lunchtime entertaining.

A perfect evening setting

A narrow-beam spotlight provides a central focus to the table. Down-lights emphasizing the corridor are dimmed to a candle-light level to create an air of intimacy.

successful
lighting for
dining rooms

decorative
lighting for a
chandelier

Chandeliers as a feature

A crystal chandelier can be a feature
object as well as a light source. Often
crystal light sources, when full on,
can create unwanted glare. A simple
step of installing a dimmer will reduce
the output of the lamps and resulting
glare so that the chandelier is more
noticeable as a decorative object.
This can be further enhanced by
installing four downlights into the
ceiling above which are used to light
the crystal itself.

Focus above a table

In this dining room, two lights
accentuate the blinds, but the main
focus is the chandelier which
provides the general light in the room.
Used on its own, the light created
would be flat and boring, but
controlled separately from all other
light sources the chandelier can be
dimmed to a candle-like glow. The
four low-voltage downlights shine
through the chandelier to throw the
flowers in the centre of the table into
dramatic relief.

Kitchens vary more in size than almost any other room, from small, functional and galley-style, to spacious, open-plan family rooms which may include sofas and a dining table. A flexible lighting scheme is required because a kitchen is not only often the centre of family life, especially if there are children, but also used for entertaining friends as well as being the place for cooking and preparing food.

kitchens

To reflect the wide range of functions which kitchens must fulfil, the lighting design should be flexible. It should adapt from a bright, general light for the day, especially in dark kitchens as a supplement to daylight, to an intimate light in the evening. As with other rooms in your house, the first thing to consider is the general lighting. In the past, bare fluorescents were often chosen as they provided a bright, diffuse light which created little shadow. However, as well as being unattractive, their light can be too harsh for evenings.

1 Low-voltage downlights are located close to the cupboard fronts to accentuate the finish, light the surface and supplement the under-cupboard lighting. By lighting the fronts of the cabinets a spacious feel is created in this kitchen.

2 With no wall-mounted cupboards, this adjustable tungsten wall light can be twisted in any direction to provide a useful task light along the work surfaces.

Low-voltage downlights emphasize the front of the cabinets, increasing a sense of space.

Fluorescent tubes are concealed behind the frosted glass splashback to light the top.

Downlights used over the cooker have sealed glass covers for easy cleaning.

The wide beam of slim cabinet lights, built into the niche, provide even light on the top shelf.

Track lighting has often been used in kitchens but is usually positioned wrongly in the centre of the room, directing light at the kitchen worktops. If your kitchen were purely for show, this would be fine. But as soon as you work at a counter, your body is positioned between the light and the surface, which creates a shadow. The track therefore needs to be located much closer to the work surface, no more than 1m (40in) away from the cupboards. More than one track will usually be required to light a kitchen adequately, and the layout of the room may even call for a square arrangement of tracks. A small, galley kitchen is the only occasion where the central track method can be used successfully: it will automatically be close to the kitchen cupboards, and the light will shine over your head at the cupboard doors, with the reflected light bouncing off to light all the kitchen worktops. An alternative to track is a wire system (see page 98). These cables appear almost invisible, and the individual bulbs can be adjusted along them to light as required.

In kitchens with low ceilings, spotlights and tracks may be unsightly and too much heat may be emitted from the bulbs themselves. Fluorescent sources can be used, but you will achieve best effects by reflecting light off other surfaces. With a high ceiling, it may be possible to conceal a fluorescent lamp on top of the cupboards to create a successful general light reflecting off the ceiling. However, using fluorescents directly as downlights can instil the atmosphere of an industrial kitchen rather than a domestic one. Their other main disadvantage is their poor quality of light compared to tungsten halogen. Fluorescent has a flat quality which gives an excellent working light, but does not bring out the best in surface finishes.

The choice of the colour of the fluorescent bulb is also important: a cool, white fluorescent light can appear too harsh while the warmer lights can appear slightly 'dirty'. Fluorescent is difficult to dim and so at night can be too harsh. If you are certain you wish to use fluorescent and would like to be able to dim the lights, you will need to power them with high-frequency, dimmable ballasts (see page 98) which can be expensive.

Tungsten halogen fittings can be used as uplights to provide the general lighting in a kitchen. They are simpler to dim than fluorescent fittings, but far less energy-efficient. Whichever you use, you will almost certainly require some form of task highlights as well, possibly over a central island or under the kitchen cabinets.

The most effective and attractive kitchen technique is to use recessed downlights arranged regularly with wide beam lamps. As well as appearing far neater than a surface-mounted track and spotlights, they are also less susceptible to the gathering of grease, dust and dirt of a surface spotlight. The usual mistake, however, is to position the downlights in the centre of the room so that they focus on the floor rather than on the perimeters of the room. Without good task lighting, the perimeter work surfaces will be poorly lit and, because the units themselves are not lit, the walls will appear dark.

With the design of modern kitchen units using natural materials or painted decorative finishes, it is best to direct the light at the front of the cabinets and units to give reflected light to your work surfaces. This has the benefit not only of directing the light where it is required, but also making the kitchen appear brighter as all the vertical surfaces are lit. The neatest downlights are low-voltage. They have the added benefit of providing a daylight quality to your lighting, which can be very important in a basement, yet when dimmed will provide a much softer light.

Task lighting in a kitchen is as important as the general lighting. If possible it should be controlled separately from the general lighting. Usually there are two main types of task lighting in a kitchen: under-cupboard lighting and the lighting of a central island. Under-cupboard lighting normally falls into three categories: fluorescent, tungsten striplight and low-voltage lighting.

Fluorescent is cool running and has a long lamp life but generally does not give the soft, intimate light which you may possibly require for a dimmed supper setting. Moreover, if your worktops are very reflective, made of polished granite or similar, fluorescent light can produce unsightly reflections.

1 The lighting on the ceiling and cornice is the diffuse 'borrowed' light from the room beyond the glass screen. A tungsten spot-light is clipped to the central stem of the island so that the beam can easily be adjusted to focus where required on the worktop.

2 A number of low-voltage bulbs on flexi-arms can be twisted in any direction, providing an unusual, decorative and functional light to this central work area. The background lighting is from tungsten lamps in large industrial-style, aluminium reflectors.

3 Recessed downlights provide an arc of light over the walls, and a ceiling pendant with a wide reflector lights the island. A further downlight highlights the stainless steel extractor fan over the cooker.

1 Halogen uplights in this high-ceilinged room provide the general light, and combine effectively with low-voltage under-counter lights, which create interesting reflections on the stainless steel.

2 A single low-voltage downlight creates emphasis on the cooker hood. The granite either side is also lit by low-voltage down-lights, but these are positioned very close to the wall.

3 The feature low-voltage up/downlights provide the in-fill lighting, whilst task light is created by discreet, built in, low voltage sources over the cooker and sink unit.

4 Fluorescent under-counter light gives a flat, even, working light, but is only successful if the worktop is non-reflective.

Tungsten striplights provide a soft glow but have several disadvantages. Because the linear tungsten filaments are fragile the bulbs tend to blow quite often, especially with frequent banging of cupboard doors. They also get quite hot, which may not be ideal if food is stored in the cupboards above.

A low-voltage under-cupboard fixture is one of the best solutions. Not only is the low-voltage light far brighter and crisper when on full than its competitors, it provides, when dimmed, a candle-like quality. Because they are only 19mm (¾in) deep, low-voltage bulbs can be recessed into the base of cupboards or surface-mounted behind a small pelmet. Their main disadvantage is that they are more expensive to install and their lamp life is shorter than a fluorescent source, but their light provides infinitely more enhancement to the work surface finish. And dimming will certainly prolong their lamp life.

The central island of a kitchen often needs additional task lighting. This can be achieved with an arrangement of downlights above it, controlled independently from all other lights in the room. Alternatively, if a hanging device for pots and pans is positioned over the island, downlights can be incorporated into this. It is best for the lighting to be located within the hanging device itself to avoid the possibility of shadows. Pendants will provide an unusual decorative effect as well as a soft focus of light over the island.

feature
lighting for
kitchen splash-
backs

Innovative task lighting

Innovative methods of task lighting include designing a frosted glass back to the cabinets, and back-lighting them with either a fluorescent or low-voltage source. Fluorescent light will give a more even effect, while low-voltage will provide an attractive scalloped design behind the glass, as shown here. The table in the foreground has low-voltage downlights cross lighting the surface as a useful task light.

Front light

The back-lighting alone puts the pans into silhouette, and a soft, low-voltage front light emphasizes the stainless steel finishes. Being controlled separately, the front light can be used independently of the back light.

Back light

The low-voltage back light is successful, as the wall behind the glass is painted white to maximize reflection. This provides an almost even light, putting all the contents of the shelves into dramatic silhouette.

In bedrooms, effective task lighting is necessary for night-time reading and around dressing tables, and the general light needs to adapt to every requirement of the changing seasons: on a dark winter morning, low-voltage bright lights will provide early risers with a feeling of get-up-and-go. The lighting should also be strong enough to distinguish between the blue and black of your clothes in the wardrobe.

bedrooms

When designing a lighting scheme for a bedroom, it is essential that each of the chosen effects is easily adjustable, according to the mood you wish to create or the brightness of light required. As this is the last room to be seen at night and the first room to be seen in the morning, you need lighting that will bring a calming atmosphere at night, with task lighting for reading and around a dressing table, as well as a refreshing wash of light when you awake.

1 A concealed linear light source built into the wall directly behind the head of the bed not only acts as an architectural delineation but also provides an effective reading light.

2 These dramatic uplights provide general light in the room and some light onto the bed. If wanting a reading light, however, it would be best to combine these with a more localized source.

For a general wash of light, particularly if your bedroom has a fairly low ceiling, downlights can be effective if they reflect their light to the walls and floor and are used in conjunction with table lamps. If bright light is unnecessary, table lamps strategically positioned around the bedroom can often be enough. This would normally consist of four fixtures, two either side of your bed and one or two on a chest of drawers or desk. In addition, you could place a standard lamp behind a chair. If your ceiling is high, however, you could consider uplighting, using wall-mounted fixtures. Halogen floodlights can be located on top of cupboards to create an almost invisible source of bright uplight, reflecting off the ceiling.

With feature lighting, unusual effects can be achieved within a bedroom. Some can be soft and subtle and some dramatic at night. You can achieve a beautifully soft glow by placing a linear light under the bed (see pages 96–7) so that the bed itself, in the centre of the room, will seem almost to float. A similar effect can be achieved by lighting under the bottom of shelves, particularly if the shelves are in a recess.

Other dramatic effects include a 'star-lit' ceiling made by small fibre optic heads only slightly piercing the ceiling and giving the impression of sleeping out under the stars. When these are switched off the ceiling appears no different to any other but, at night-time, with the lights on, it gives the effect of numerous small stars.

More familiar feature lighting effects also work well in bedrooms, and may be appropriate with the style of room and decoration. You could possibly light a picture, either over the bed or over a fireplace if you have one, use uplighting under a bay window to highlight your curtains, or choose favourite ornaments to become your lighting focus.

When the general and feature lighting is decided, the task lighting must be considered. For a dressing table, you will achieve the most flattering facial light by placing lights either side of the mirror. An ideal solution is to use two separate lamps. It is important that the shades are not coloured so that a natural light will be thrown onto your face.

An efficient reading light is essential in a bedroom. The ultimate in bedroom task lights, used in conjunction with bedside table lamps, is the fibre optic flexi-light. This is fixed to the wall at shoulder height and provides a completely flexibly positioned bright reading light. The fibre optic light box (see page 98) would be located under the bed.

A more traditional source of reading light are table lamps on either side of the bed, but they must be placed in the correct position if eyestrain and awkward body positioning are to be avoided. If lamps are located on a bedside table, the light is often in the wrong place, almost forcing you to lean out of bed to read. You need to achieve the right balance between the size of the lamp and the height of the table. If the table is too high, the glare of the lamp will shine into your eyes and the spread of light will be too wide. The ideal height for the base of the shade is at shoulder level when you are sitting up in bed.

An alternative to table lamps is an adjustable wall light on an extendible bracket (see page 98) with arm extensions. As this is wall-mounted, you can control the precise height and position of the lamp, but you will need to know the height and size of the bed before installation.

If you want to create a pool of light purely for reading, and your ceiling is not too high, an effective solution is to use a low-voltage spotlight with a narrow-beam lamp on a dimmer. Again, before installation you will need to be certain of your reading position in bed so that the spotlight is placed in the correct area on the ceiling.

Task lighting is also necessary for a wardrobe. Low-voltage downlights, with frosted lenses, can be used to provide a soft wash over the front of cabinets. A concealed linear strip could be used above a wardrobe, or door-operated lighting (see page 98) could be installed for automatic light.

In most bedrooms you will need at least two switchlines (see page 98) to control your different light sources: one for bedside lamps and one for other lamps. If you are using either uplights or downlights, these will need a third switch. With a double bed, it may be easier to control each bedside light individually, which will add another switchline. Two-way switching to the bedside works well, as all lights can be turned on and off from the bed. A dimmer, either by the door or at the side of the bed, will give easy control.

1 These wardrobes are lit by a concealed linear, low-voltage, tungsten source in a trough mounted at the junction between wall and ceiling to provide a soft, continuous wash of light. The light in this room is for decorative purposes but also helps with task requirements when clothes need to be found.

2 In a room which has a rush of natural light, keeping all walls and surfaces plain white will allow for ultimate reflection. Here, the wardrobes are lit from behind, casting the objects within into silhouette and creating an unusual feature.

reading
lights in the
bedroom

Downlights

Low-voltage downlights with a well-recessed light source can be controlled individually (by switches placed on each side of the bed) to provide effective reading lights for both sides of the bed. They also offer a wash of general light to the rest of the room.

Fibre optics

The ultimate fibre optic bedside light, built into this headboard, provides a dedicated reading light and, as its beam is so precise, will literally light only your book. The table lamp adds a softness to the atmosphere of the room when ambient light is required.

Wall lights

These two wall-mounted bedside lights create good reading light on either side of the bed. They are at the correct height to light over the shoulder when you are reading in bed, and are low enough to ensure that the light source is still concealed.

Until fairly recently bathrooms were designed as purely functional rooms, but in contemporary homes they have taken on a new role as a sanctuary of relaxation. There is often little natural light in a bathroom, so your lighting design needs to complement the style of the room and be flexible enough to change from bright and invigorating in the morning to a softer, more subdued ambience for evening baths.

bathrooms

The location of your light fixtures is crucial within a bathroom, partly because of the potential safety hazards, but also because many of the surface finishes are very reflective. Crisp, low-voltage halogen light reflects particularly well off these surfaces, and its success has given rise to a range of new lighting techniques. Instead of a regular grid of downlights in the ceiling, you could consider locating the lights directly over your basin and bath; when they are filled, a wonderful pattern of rippling water will be reflected across the ceiling.

1 Recessed low-voltage fixtures uplight the thick glass vanity top and emphasize the textured glass surface. A purely decorative effect, this needs to be combined with a practical downlight for lighting the face.

2 A low-voltage downlight catches the glass screen at the end of the bath and highlights the chrome tap. Other downlights, close to the glass walls at the back of the room, provide an arc of light to wash the walls and floor.

If you do not want downlights directly overhead and the bath is against a wall, you could position a series of small low-voltage downlights in the ceiling, approximately 100mm (4in) from the wall. This will create a beautiful scalloped pattern, suggesting water streaming down the tiles, and is also a good way of lighting a shower unit.

As well as the practicalities of your bathroom lighting you will need to consider your feature elements. For example, if there is a niche for ornaments, a small downlight could be installed within this to highlight objects on a shelf or to light all the way through if the shelving unit is glass.

By lighting underneath the bath, it can appear almost to float. A soft ropelight (see page 97) concealed beneath the bath surround will give a continuous soft, even glow and could almost be used as a nightlight because of its low brightness. Alternatively, a small spotlight could be recessed around the base of the bath to skim out across the floor in strong shafts of light. This is a dramatic effect which can look magnificent in a modern bathroom. To achieve this successfully, it is essential that you use a fully-sealed low-voltage baffled light of no more than 12w 12v; any higher and the heat of the fitting could scald your feet.

1 Lights located close to the back wall create a scalloped pattern down the wall. For best results these should be no more than 100mm (4in) from the wall to ensure that the arc of light is high on the wall.

2 A continuous fluorescent strip of light is used both above and below the mirror. The light below emphasizes the marble surfaces, and the light above creates a general, daytime wash which is also an excellent, shadow-free, general light for the face.

3 Low-voltage downlights are located close to the rear wall of the shower, whilst two fixtures are directed down onto the bath, making it a sculptural focal point within the bathroom.

If your basin is made of glass, recessing an uplight below it creates a stunning effect, making the basin appear to be lit internally. This will need to be balanced by a downlight or your face will appear rather ghostly. The uplight should be fully sealed and the beam of the lamp wide enough to ensure maximum coverage of the glass bowl itself.

If you control each area of your lighting separately it will be more adaptable to your changing needs. Dimming your lighting will make it work at all times of the day from the 'full on' effect in the morning to the soft, subdued effect in the evening, which you may wish to combine with candles.

The position of dimmer switches depends on the local regulations of the country and should be checked before wiring to the inside or outside of the bathroom. In the UK, switches must be placed outside your bathroom unless you choose to have a pull-cord inside the bathroom. The main problem with pull-cords is that they cannot be dimmed and, if you have more than one switchline (see page 98) for your different lighting techniques, you will need two or three pull-cords, which is both impractical and unattractive.

Before planning any work in the bathroom it is best to consult a professional electrician regarding safety regulations.

Tungsten wash

Unless a shower is properly lit there is a danger that it will become an unattractive dark hole in your bathroom. Fortunately, there is a wide range of fully water-resistant fittings now available which cater to all tastes and demands.

Here, the grey concrete shower is lit by a simple tungsten bulkhead. Further natural light is filtered into the space through a textured glass wall on one side, creating reflections on the opposite side. The warmth of the tungsten light, in its perfect circular fixture, provides a very warm, diffuse light on the wooden shower fittings, and contrasts with the diffused light through the glass wall.

Scalloped downlights

The scalloping effect of low-voltage downlights works particularly well in showers, as it helps to draw your eye towards the rear wall and gives the impression of extra space. Alternatively, lights recessed into the side wall of a shower, using a directional spreader lens (see page 98), will deflect the light to the rear walls. You should aim to direct the light down onto the back wall; their visual appearance on the side wall will suggest a number of portholes. The spreader lenses are usually part of the fixture itself or in some cases can be ordered as a special attachment.

Here, the two low-voltage downlights reflect off the blue tiled wall of the shower to provide a strong focal point within the bathroom.

Note: In bathrooms, safety is of great importance, as water and electricity are not a very good combination! Low-voltage light sources are ideal, as 12v reduces almost all of the hazards of mains-voltage fittings. A glass cover over the lamp fitting is, however, recommended in case they are splashed: halogen bulbs can, on very rare occasions, shatter, and a glass cover will protect you from any accidents.

ways
to light
showers

Recessed mirror light

One of the priorities in a bathroom is the lighting around the mirror. If this is done badly, your face will either be completely in shadow or have unsightly dark shadows cast across it. A single low-voltage downlight positioned over the basin looks magnificent but casts shadows on the features of anyone looking into the mirror. A single downlight source can, however, be supplemented with other lighting effects. For example, if the downlight is directed slightly towards the mirror, as here, the reflected light will be more diffuse and reduce the shadowing.

If the basin is a light colour then the downlight will be reflected back up and increase the general effect. The ideal solution is to have side lighting from a diffuse source on either side of the mirror, or, even better, as a continuous strip around the mirror as shown here. This achieves virtually no shadowing and gives the most even modelling of the face.

ways
to light
a mirror

Concealed lighting

General lighting here is created by the back-lighting of the glass in the niche, combined with the downlights washing the front of the frosted glass behind the mirror. The specific highlight to the face is from a tungsten light concealed within the mirror.

Strip lights

In this bathroom, two tungsten strip lights provide a soft, even light to the face whilst the low-voltage downlights, centred on each basin, emphasize the surface colour and texture. If the downlight alone is used, shadow will be created on the face.

More and more people are now working from home, either from a desk area in the corner of a living room or bedroom, or in a separate office. Working for long periods of time, particularly on a computer, demands specific lighting solutions so that the right environment for focused work is created, and headaches and eyestrain are avoided. If the work space is part of another room then flexibility is essential.

work areas

Unlike most other rooms, the most important requirement when lighting a work area is an effective task light. A successful balance must be achieved between this and the general lighting to avoid eyestrain, which can result from the contrast between a well-lit surface and dark surrounding walls, or if too much light is reflecting onto a screen. Feature lighting is not essential, but will be effective in creating more atmosphere in a room where you have to spend time, and could be used to highlight a bookshelf or a picture.

1 An adjustable table lamp allows great control over the direction of light over the desk. Three low-voltage downlights, recessed into the ceiling, also provide general light directly onto the working area, separating it from other parts of the room.

2 The same space by day, with natural light filtered through the Venetian blinds allowing enough light onto the desk

Task lighting could be provided by a desk lamp or, if there are shelves above the desk, by lighting fixed to, or underneath, the shelves. Desk lamps and those fixed to shelves offer a degree of adaptability as the direction of their light beam can be adjusted. A movable light would work very well if a computer is to be used, since the amount of light and any reflection on the screen can be fully controlled. Whichever solution is chosen, the task light should, if possible, be on a separate switch from all other sources in the room so that it creates a focus on the work area only.

The general lighting is probably most efficiently provided by a free-standing uplight, which will create a soft,

diffuse light without casting problematic reflections on the computer screen; these reflections can occur when using downlights in your overall scheme.

If the room has shelves, further sources can be employed. If there is a gap of at least 600mm (24in) between the top shelf and the ceiling, an uplight could be incorporated above the shelf. If the gap is smaller than 600mm (24in), a continuous source, such as overlapping fluorescent tubes or xenon striplights, will be more successful than a tungsten halogen uplight, which would create a 'hotspot' of intense light on the ceiling rather than provide a general wash over the room.

If you have a whole wall of shelving or a library, low-voltage track lighting will give enough light for you to see every book on each shelf. Alternatively, traditional library lights can be employed. Sometimes also called French library lights, these are usually wall-mounted on brackets, and can have one-, two- or three-arm connections depending on the extension and versatility required. Originating from the idea of a candle on a vertical pole, with an arm-extension so that the lamp could be shifted upwards or sideways, they offer a focused light that can be moved across the shelves. The electrical versions provide the same versatility for both contemporary and traditional interiors.

1   A home office, with two adjustable table-mounted lamps for the desk area to provide task light when necessary. Shelf-mounted lights create general light in the room but can also be adjusted to become task lights on the shelves.

2   A table lamp with a wide reflector and pale shade gives a wash of light over the desk for letter writing. General light is provided by sources in other areas of the room.

3   A number of light sources create a good general light in this office, with a combination of table lamps, ceiling pendant and a free-standing lamp for extra light when required.

Your garden can be such a pleasure during the day, but is it forgotten at night? Even if it is small, a garden could become an extra room in your house, and provide an added dimension to the character of your home. If your garden has a well-designed lighting scheme, your eye will be drawn outside to all the features you have lit, and the feeling of space will expand to include the area surrounding your home.

gardens

A garden can appear magical at night by simply lighting a few carefully chosen features. Even a lantern in a small summer house can be enough to provide a glow or focus. A little light goes a long way at night; it is therefore important to decide what features to light and to what intensity.

Garden lighting can be problematic. One example of this is the 'security light' approach, where a halogen light located above a door or window gives an overall flood of light, but will not create any atmospheric or feature lighting.

1 Candles define the edges of this veranda but table and standard lamps are brought out with the furniture to create a room outside. It is always worth positioning sockets to allow for temporary lighting on verandas used as outdoor seating areas.

2 An urn in the distance is a striking focus when lit; here, the light stone contrasts brightly against the dark green hedging. A small concealed halogen flood is located approximately 1m (40in) in front of the urn and lights the structure evenly.

This use of a single halogen light source is tolerable when the garden is viewed from inside, though it does give a rather flat light. However, when you sit in the garden it is intolerable to look at, creating glare and an unwelcoming harshness.

As with interiors, exterior lighting can be broken down into various functions. For example, lighting pathways, defining an entrance, lighting a vista or a feature, lighting a terrace for dining, and security.

The first priority for landscape lighting is to identify the main features you wish to light; this can vary from a landscape item such as a tree or shrub, or an architectural feature such as a pergola, statue, folly or arch. Your method of lighting will vary depending on the feature. As with interior lighting, the key to successful lighting is to conceal the light

source so, unless you wish to make a feature of the lamp itself, you only see the lighting effect. For example, a folly, bridge or summer house at the end of a garden could be lit with a small floodlight as long as this feature was only viewed from one direction. If the garden is used at night, then this approach could create unwanted glare from some approaches, so more discreet lighting would be required.

Garden light fittings generally tend to be black, but the neatest ones to look out for are those finished in dark green, as they blend in with the foliage more effectively. Copper fittings can be similarly effective as they will patinate to a natural green colour with age. Bronze fittings are also suitable, particularly if they are mounted in a tree, as they blend in with the colour of the trunk.

1 These wall lights are simple, yet their effect is dramatic. A single light source has been cleverly fitted with a special directional lens to throw a narrow shaft of light upwards, and a wide beam downwards, over this outdoor patio area.

2 The background lighting on this terrace is created by miniature, green, low-voltage, spiked uplights which light the trunks of each copper beech tree and catch the foliage around. The spill of light is reflected off the perimeter white walls. Two further spotlights at the planting edge, concealed by two of the pots, are directed towards the large corner pot, to create front lighting. Candles have also been chosen to help set the mood.

3 This door is framed by the large, pyramidal structures with tungsten par 38 spotlights within. The light sources shine through the metal frames of the fittings to cast a wonderful pattern across the back wall.

Topiary

Putting trees into silhouette is an effective way of lighting them, so in some instances they may be a specific feature but, in others, their shape and form are defined by lighting the walls or buildings behind. I rarely use coloured lamps in gardens as I feel that plants have enough natural colour. It is best to highlight plants using a white light to bring out their true colour during the changing seasons.

Here an up/downlight has been used which creates a feature of the light source as well as a dramatic silhouette of the tree. The base of the tree is highlighted with four small, green, low-voltage spiked lights, with a transformer, located under the base of the wooden pot.

Low-level plants and stone

Statues are often best lit using a small spiked spotlight concealed by local foliage. If lighting a statue in the centre of a lawn, then a fully-recessed adjustable uplight would be the most discreet solution, which also avoids problems when mowing the lawn. Low-level shrubbery is a useful way to conceal a light fixture, but can still allow the light to filter through as long as the foliage around the light fixture is trimmed regularly. Here, candles light each step and two spiked uplights are used, one uplighting the tree and the other highlighting the well.

ways
to light
a garden
feature

Lighting a trellis and path

Lighting a trellis can create a wonderful effect, not only by lighting the foliage that grows up it, but by accentuating the trellis design. A diamond-shaped trellis, for example, will create a strong diagonal pattern; by highlighting the foliage you can slightly soften this strong architectural effect.

Paths, steps and terraces need to be illuminated to provide easy access from your house to the garden or from one part of the garden to another. One way of lighting a path is to rely on reflected light provided by lighting features such as planting or trees. This is normally adequate to light a level path, but special attention needs to be made to light any changes in level. A small spotlight could be located in a tree, lighting downwards using the 'moonlighting' method (see page 98) or a localized source can be built into the step or be provided by a small, copper, 'mushroom'-style fixture or various types of bollard light (see page 98). These should be green, if possible, to blend in with the foliage.

Here, the path and trellis have been lit using a garland of fairy lights wound around both the low-level box hedging and the trellis arch.

Lighting a pergola and trees

A pergola provides another interesting structure for lighting. Normally, it covers a walkway leading to a feature which could be lit to provide a strong visual focus. A pergola could be uplit, highlighting the framework as well as lighting the canopy. A small spot could be concealed at a high level to light down through, or across, the foliage at canopy level. Up/downlight sources could also be mounted half way up the pergola to create more definition.

Just as for interior lighting, a fixture with a baffled light source or a fixture with a cowl attachment (see page 98) is most appropriate so that the light source can be concealed and the effect of the light maximized.

Concealing lights up the tree trunk can be a very effective way of lighting a tree with a large canopy. Tungsten halogen or metal halide sources can be effective; but it is recommended that some form of baffle or glare shield is used. Invariably the fitting will need to be tilted out to light the canopy fully, and 'barn door' attachments (see page 98) can be used to conceal the light source. With this method there is less likelihood of the effect becoming overgrown and lost.

Here, small, green, 50w 12v reflectors throw light across the path, whilst three 50w 12v spiked spotlights emphasize the ladder and tree beyond the table.

3

practicalities

Planning your lighting

Before embarking on a new electrical installation it is worth having your existing wiring and fuse box checked. Very old houses will probably not have the power capacity required and may need to be rewired. Fuses that continually blow are a good indication of an over-loaded system. Modern lighting techniques require more sockets and outlets compared to the old 'single pendant in the centre of the room' approach. This may involve wiring a separate switchline back to the distribution board to take the additional load. For any installation it is always best to use a qualified electrician. Electricity is potentially dangerous, and for this reason installing wiring and light fittings is subject to strict safety regulations which need to be adhered to. These vary from country to country, but a qualified electrician will be well aware of the requirements.

Checklist of things to do before planning your lighting

1. Start by making a sketch plan of the room to scale, putting all the furniture and key pictures in position. Note all the existing power points, as some of these could be re-used.

2. Think about the activities that will be taking place in the room and how much general light and task light they will require.

3. Decide which light sources and techniques to use for the general light and where they should be placed for best effect. Note that a pale interior will reflect more light than a dark interior.

4. Make a note on the plan of the position of any feature light sources and what these sources will be. If using downlights to light an object on a wall, remember that the height of the ceiling will determine how far from the wall the fitting should be positioned.

5. Once you have established the various lighting types, it is useful to consider how they will be controlled. A good system will separately switch or dim each lighting element in a room.

Checklist of things to consider when undertaking a new installation

1. Ensure that you have enough sockets in the room. Ideally, use 5 amp sockets for any lamps and allow 13 amp sockets for a TV, stereo, computer, vacuum cleaner, etc. There is no need to double up; just select the appropriate socket for the appropriate place. Trailing flexes may cause accidents, so if possible install floor sockets in the centre of the room for greater flexibility when placing lamps next to seats or tables.

2. The positioning of all light fittings is crucial. Scorch marks can result if fittings, particularly uplights, are located too near the ceiling or flammable materials. The fitting usually has a minimum safe distance written within its installation instructions, but if not you should consult the manufacturer.

3. Recessed uplights installed in floors can get very hot unless fibre optics are used (which are very expensive). The position of these uplights therefore needs to be considered carefully. Their use should be limited to feature lighting which can be switched off if children or pets will be in the room.

4. If you want to install recessed downlights, check there is a ceiling void and how deep this is. It is also important to know what the ceiling is made of, whether standard plasterboard or a mix of lathe and plaster. The fixing clips of any fixture will need to be checked to ensure they are compatible with the ceiling type.

5. Check if the ceiling void is full of insulation. If it is, clean it out around the the position of the light to prevent overheating.

6. Check the local fire officer's requirements and establish whether a fire box is required over any of the fittings.

7. Check the position of switches for ease of use. If you are changing the way a door swings, remember to change the position of the switch.

8. For exterior installations, ensure that all cables are mounted well away from any areas that may need digging or regular mowing. If cables are located in the centre of a garden, they should be a minimum of 450mm (1¾in) underground. Check that all equipment is weatherproof and suitable for exterior use.

1 At high level, a narrow-beam, low-voltage spotlight highlights the table in this courtyard. A visual focus is created by the dramatic up/downlight on the back wall of the interior.

Control

Once you have established the various types of lighting, it is useful to consider how they will be controlled. A good system will separately switch or dim each lighting element in a room. The first stage is to switch each effect or element separately, i.e. the general lighting separately from the feature lighting and task lighting. This gives a degree of adaptability over the balance of light, and the subsequent change in mood, which will be useful in most rooms. A further advantage of using dimmers is that they extend the life of filament bulbs including tungsten, tungsten halogen and low-voltage light sources.

A dimmer has a maximum load which cannot be exceeded, and so the correct size must be used for the amount of light sources you wish to dim. It should also be noted that a dimmer has a minimum load rating; if this is not reached the light source may flicker. The most usual dimmer is the rotary (turning) type, but there are also sliders and touch-plate controls. As the dimmer is working it may emit a low hum. If you are sensitive to this, it is worth considering locating the dimmer outside the room or using a pre-set dimmer system. If the hum is very loud there may be a fault with the dimmer module itself, which can be checked by an electrician.

With standard dimming, the lights can only be dimmed from one position, so with two-way switching you will only be able to switch the lights on or off at the level to which they were previously set. It is therefore important to consider the best location for the dimmer switch.

Pre-set lighting is commonly used in hotels, but is becoming increasingly popular in the home as it removes the need for a bank of four to six dimmer knobs and large plates in a room. The plate usually has four scenes (buttons) offering pre-set 'moods' and an off button. For each 'mood' the lighting has effectively been pre-set to suit that particular time of day. It is similar to having to adjust the levels of each light source manually and then memorizing that exact dimmed level. Most pre-sets also offer a raise and lower facility so that the scene can be further dimmed, if required, without losing the original setting.

In a living room typical settings would be:

Scene 1   Bright – daytime
Scene 2   Softer – early evening
Scene 3   More dramatic – after dinner
Scene 4   TV mode

In a kitchen/breakfast room:

Scene 1   Bright, daylight feel
Scene 2   Focused over worktops for cooking
Scene 3   Dinner setting with kitchen worktops low
Scene 4   Low level, for quick visits to the kitchen during the day

Photocell control

A photocell instructs the lights to come on when it is dark.; it is recommended for all garden installations as it prevents the lights being accidentally switched on during the day. Once switched on they will remain off during the day, only coming on when it is dark. They can easily be switched on or off at any time when required.

PIR

A PIR is a passive infra-red detector that switches a light on when it detects movement, and is best linked to a photocell to prevent daytime operation. It is particularly useful when used to control entrance and security lights, switching the lights on for a set length of time (about 2–3 minutes) and then switching off again. It is recommended that these sensors have an override on/off switch, so that if used in conjunction with security lights they can be switched off when necessary.

Timeclock

A timeclock can set your lights to come on and go off again at specific times of the day, and are often used in conjunction with photocells. They can also be linked into a pre-set control system, so that different scenes can be switched on and off when the house is empty to make it appear as if someone is there.

Fixtures

Baffles

A baffle is a device, usually a metal or wood shield, attached to a light fitting to conceal the bulb from direct view, which helps to prevent glare. When designing a baffle to conceal a light source, you must consider all viewing angles, particularly when locating fittings at the side of a cabinet, in shelves or under cupboards, etc. It is important to include a return baffle when a light source is used in shelves. to conceal the light source completely on both sides as well as from the front, so that from any angle you will only be aware of the effect of light on the shelves rather than being distracted by the light itself.

Lampshades

The design of lampshade you choose will have an impact on your overall lighting scheme, as different shades have different impacts. A light-coloured shade will provide good side lighting to the face. A parchment or silk shade gives a soft side light, whereas a solid card shade provides an up-and-downlight effect. If the inside of the shade is gold, the light reflected will be much warmer than if it is silver or white. Some old standard lamps may have up to three bulbs, two acting as downlights and one as an uplight by the addition of a simple white cone around it. This is a good idea not often seen today.

A combination of several lamps will help to create successful lighting. It is worthwhile introducing a lamp switchline, whether 2 or 5 amps, so that all the lamps can easily be switched on or off at the door, rather than at each lamp individually.

1 This miniature low-voltage downlight, used in a display cabinet, has an integral baffle to reduce the direct view of the bulb. This allows a focused beam of light to shine through the glass decanter and down onto shelves beneath.

Light bulbs (lamps)

There is a huge range of bulbs available. Some fixtures will require more specialist bulbs to achieve the desired effect. If this is the case, the manufacturer will specify which bulb is required. The main varieties of bulbs are described below, along with an indication of whether they are mains-voltage (operating at 240v), or low-voltage (operating at 12v/24v and therefore requiring a transformer):

Tungsten lamps (GLS) [240v]

These have a tungsten filament and are mostly used in table lamps and wall lights. They come in a variety of shapes and sizes and usually have two types of bases: Edison Screw (ES) or Bayonet Cap (BC). The fitting will specify which type of bulb is required, although only the ES fitting is available in America.

1 The pearl bulb, which has a milky white appearance, gives a softer light. If clear bulbs are used, for example in a table lamp, patterns and shadows of the lamp shade will be produced by the filament of the bulb on the ceiling, but when using a pearl bulb these shadows will not occur as the light is softer.

2 Variations on the clear bulb include the crown silvered bulb. These are useful when installed in low pendants over tables, as the light is reflected back into the shade, reducing direct glare. They can also be used in large parabolic spot-lights, which have now largely been replaced by low-voltage fixtures.

Bayonet Cap (BC) fitting

Edison Screw (ES) fitting

Candle lamps [240v]

3 These are tungsten bulbs moulded into the shape of a candle, and are available in both pearl and clear glass. They are also available in twisted shapes for chandeliers. Once again, for small wall lights with shades, use pearl candle bulbs to avoid creating shadows, but in wall lights, lanterns and chandeliers where the bare bulb is visible use a clear bulb as the visible tungsten filament sparkles off the glass, and when dimmed emulates candle light. When undimmed these sources can create glare.

Clear candle lamp

Twisted candle lamp

4 *Miniature candle lamps [240v]* (not illustrated)

These are primarily used in chandeliers, lanterns and some wall lights where the appearance of a real candle is required. This small light source is far more elegant and creates less glare than a standard candle bulb and is the most suitable source when a visible bulb is required.

Mains-voltage halogen [240v]

These bulbs have a long tungsten filament surrounded by halogen gas to make the light that is emitted much whiter.

5 The single-ended version can replace standard GLS bulbs, for example in a basement where a whiter light is required. These could also be used in table lamps to give the room an instant lift and create a daylight effect.

6 The double-ended variety are usually used in wall-mounted and free-standing halogen uplights as well as exterior security floodlights.

Reflector spotlight (ISL) [240v]

7 ISL stands for internally-silvered lamps, and the type includes flood reflector lamps. These are typically used in small mains-voltage downlights and spotlights, but the use of low-voltage and miniature mains-voltage bulbs is gradually limiting their use. Various wattages and sizes are available.

Par 38 [240v]

8 This is the original mains-voltage spotlight, available in either tungsten or tungsten halogen. Its large size has meant that it has gradually been superseded by low-voltage halogen and smaller mains-voltage Par 20 bulbs. It is now primarily used as a spotlight, particularly in gardens. Various wattages and sizes are available.

Low-voltage halogen capsule [12v or 24v]

9 This is a tiny compact bulb. As it operates at a lower voltage, its filament has been reduced to such a size to enable a small capsule to surround it. The grease from fingers can reduce its lamp life and thus it should not be handled with bare hands. It can be used by itself in a fitting to create a starlight effect or with a reflector to focus the light emitted from the filament in a particular arrangement. Various wattages are available.

Compact fluorescent [240v]

10 These sources have miniaturized over the years and have been re-shaped as far as possible to match the GLS bulbs, both in size and the lamp holder it fits into. They can therefore act as a direct energy-efficient swap, but care must be taken as these bulbs are not currently dimmable.

Low-voltage halogen dichroic reflector lamps [12v]

11 This takes the small low-voltage capsule bulb and includes an integral dichroic reflector which focuses its light in a number of beam widths – narrow, medium and flood. The dichroic nature of the reflector directs light forward and draws some heat back, creating a concentrated, slightly cooler beam of light. It is ideal for use in display lighting, and the flood versions of the bulb can be used in small fittings for general downlighting. Various wattages are available operating at 12v. Two sizes are most common, 50mm (2in) diameter (MR16) and 35mm (1½in) diameter (MR11).

Fibre optics (not illustrated)

These are increasingly becoming an important display lighting tool. They have been used for some time in museums because they cause no damage to valuable exhibits; although expensive, they have the major advantage of emitting no ultraviolet rays and no heat. Recent developments in both lenses and quality fibre optic cable have helped make fibre optics more versatile. They are not a light source as such, but use either a metal halide or tungsten halogen source which, with a special reflector, focuses at the end of a group of glass fibres to produce light. The glass fibres are sheathed in black and the light is transmitted down them to be emitted at the end. The light source itself is therefore remote, which can help with maintenance.

Fluorescent strips [240v]

12 These have been developed into slimmer and smaller lengths. They can be used as uplights, uplighting from the top of a kitchen cabinet, for edge lighting or local task lighting, where a cool light source is required. They can be dimmed, but do require a special ballast (see pp98–9). When dimmed they become less bright but do not become warmer in colour like the tungsten light sources. They have a very long lamp life, and should always be used with a high-frequency ballast to avoid a flickering effect as they are switched both on and off.

Architectural tubes [240v]

13 These are a tungsten alternative to fluorescent tubes. The light is softer, but the lamp life is shorter as the bulb filament is very fragile. The bulb is easily dimmable and can be used for soft uplighting effects. They can, for example, be used in areas where one part of a ceiling is raised and the light source can be concealed by a cornice, or can be used as a soft under-counter light or positioned on a mirror to provide side lighting to the face.

Track lighting/Clickstrip [12v or 24v]

14 This is a small, flexible, mini track into which low-voltage bulbs can be set. The bulbs can be positioned at various intervals – every 50mm (2in), 100mm (4in) or more. They use small low-voltage 3W, 5W, 8.5W or 10W bulbs, and the transformers needed to feed these bulbs should be calculated accordingly. This fitting is ideal for display lighting in open shelves, cornice uplighting or wherever a strip of light is required.

Ropelight/Lightstream [240v and 12v]

15 This is a run of small 'pea' bulbs set into a flexible rubber covering. A simple mains-voltage rope light is fairly small and has a long lamp life of 10,000 hours, approximately five years of normal use, after which the whole strip would need to be replaced. This is available is both low-voltage and mains-voltage versions and is ideal for the soft delineation of features, whether creating a floating effect under a bed or lighting a book shelf. This fitting has to be ordered to a precise size and is attached with a combination of double-sided tape and fixing clips.

Glossary

baffle Device attached to a light fitting that helps to prevent glare. The source of light is set back behind the tube so that it is concealed from view.

ballast This is used to provide the correct start-up current for a fluorescent tube or compact. If a ballast is high frequency this means the bulb is switched on immediately and avoids the flicker. If fluorescents are to be dimmed it is necessary to ensure the ballast is dimmable and specify this (usually they are not).

bollard lights Low-level post light which has a similar purpose to a pathlight but is tougher and more sturdy than the pathlight. Often used in commercial situations.

cowl attachment Attachment to reduce the glare from a fixture.

cross lighting Way of accenting a picture, plant or ornament by lighting it from two different directions so that the beams of light overlap on the object.

dichroic lamp (MR type) Bulb which has a reflector designed to pass the majority of its heat output backwards, in the opposite direction to the beam of light.

directional source Light fitting that casts light in a specific direction; usually mounted or recessed into the ceiling, they can be tilted for extra adaptability.

discharge sources Low-energy, high-output light source, e.g. metal halide or sodium, which has a few seconds start-up time. Used mainly in street lighting and stadiums.

door-operated switch Switch set inside a door of a piece of furniture (mainly wardrobes and fridges) which automatically turns the light on when the door is opened.

drum-shaped uplights Compact low-intensity uplight, primarily intended for feature lighting. Often used under plants or in the corners of room.

electrical outlet (5 amp etc) Device into which an electrical plug can be inserted in order to make a connection in a switchline.

extendible bracket Bracket made with two or three sections that can either be folded back on itself or extended to provide a long arm.

festoon lamp Small low-voltage tungsten bulb approximately 40mm (1½in) in size and used in a clickstrip to light shelves.

filament Thin wire (usually tungsten) inside a light bulb that heats up to provide light.

flexi-arm Adjustable arm, usually made of metal links, which can be adjusted to light in almost any direction. Ideal when used for a task light.

lamp beam width Measure of the spread of illumination obtained from a reflector as part of a bulb or fitting [narrow 14°, medium 27° or wide 40°].

lenses Accessories used to achieve different effects from the same fitting.

> **spreader lens** Accessory used to achieve an elongated beam of light when used in conjunction with a narrow-beam bulb.
>
> **frosted lens** Accessory used to achieve a more even wash of light.

metal reflector lamp Bulb which has a solid reflector to direct light and heat forward (unlike a dichroic which sends some of the heat backwards).

'moonlighting' Technique used in exterior lighting where the lights are installed at high level in a tree to filter down through the leaves to create a 'moonlight' effect.

pathlights Usually mounted on a stem, this fitting has a bulb positioned underneath a 'hat' or top which reflects the light down, e.g. 'mushroom' type.

pelmet The baffle usually built below a cabinet to conceal a light source.

projecting the light (pictures) Low-voltage fitting which is specially designed for accent lighting; it has a system of lenses and shutters that can shape the light beam to the exact outline of the picture or object being lit.

reflector This can form part of a bulb or a fitting and is used to direct light in a specific beam. Can be designed to provide either a narrow or wide distribution of light.

recessed fitting Very discreet fitting that can be positioned within the ceiling, floor or wall, flush with the level of the surface, instead of being mounted on top of the surface.

shuttering devices (barn door attachments etc.) Metal attachments on a fixture which help to control the spread of light.

spiked lights Variety of outdoor fittings which come with a spike to be inserted into the ground. As they can be placed anywhere in a garden the fittings are very flexible.

switchline Here it is used to mean the various fittings which are connected to one switch or dimmer, i.e. all fittings on one switchline operate together at the same level.

transformer Device that reduces the domestic electricity supply from mains voltage to the required low voltage.

remote light box Used for fibre optics, the light source is within a box where a reflector focuses the light to the end of the glass fibres.

UV (ultraviolet) Part of the electromagnetic spectrum. Can be harmful to artwork: lenses are available to help reduce these rays.

Wire system Type of track with two tensioned cables, powered at 12v, carrying the current to small low-voltage fittings placed between the cables.

Suppliers

These suppliers are open
to the public.

* Specialised lighting
  design service offered.

Contemporary

Aero
96 Westbourne Grove
London W2 5RT
T: 020 7221 1950
www.aerofurniture.com
• *Contemporary European
lighting*

Aram Designs
3 Kean Street
London WC2B 4AT
T: 020 7240 3933
• *Designs for home and office*

Atrium
Centrepoint
22–24 St Giles High Street
London WC2H 8LN
T: 020 7379 7288
all@atrium.com
• *Lighting by contemporary
designers*

Candela Ltd
51 Abbey Business Centre
Ingate Place
London SW8 3NS
T: 020 7720 4480
• *Range of low-voltage
downlights*

The Conran Shop
Michelin House
81 Fulham Road
London SW3 6RD
T: 020 7589 7401
conranshop@dial.pipex.com
• *Excellent range of lights*

Donghia
23 The Design Centre
Chelsea Harbour
London SW10 0XE
T: 020 7823 3456
• *Chandeliers, table and
floor lamps*

*Designer Light Shop
4 Kennington Road
London SE1 7BL
T: 020 7928 0097
• *Stylish European lighting*

Habitat
196 Tottenham Court Road
London W1P 9LD
T: 020 7631 3880
  0845 6010740 for branches
customerrelations@
  habitat.co.uk
• *Affordable stylish range*

Heals
196 Tottenham Court Road
London W1P 9LD
T: 020 7896 7555
• *Affordable stylish range*

IKEA UK Ltd
2 Drury Way
North Circular Road
London NW10 0TH
T: 020 8208 5600 for branches
• *Wide range of modern and
traditional designs*

*John Cullen Lighting
585 Kings Road
London SW6 2EH
T: 020 7371 5400
design@
  johncullenlighting.co.uk
• *Discreet lighting for house
and garden*

London Lighting
  Company
135 Fulham Road
London SW3 6RT
T: 020 7589 3612
• *A wide range of modern
lights*

Lipp
118a Holland Park Avenue
London W11 4UA
T: 020 7243 2432
• *Contemporary and classic
lights*

Mr Light
275 Fulham Road
London SW10 9PZ
T: 020 7352 7525
• *Contemporary and traditional
fittings*

Nice House
Italian Centre Courtyard
Ingram Street
Glasgow
Scotland G1 1DN
T: 0141 533 1377
• *Stylish modern lighting*

Purves & Purves
80–81 Tottenham Court Road
London W1P 9HD
T: 020 7580 8223
• *European contemporary
lighting*

*SKK
34 Lexington Street
London W1R 3HR
T: 020 7434 4095
skk@easynet.co.uk
• *Assortment of modern
designs*

Space
214 Westbourne Grove
London W11 2RH
T: 020 7229 6533
• *Cutting-edge lighting designs*

Viaduct
1–10 Summer's Street
London EC1R 5BD
T: 020 7278 8456
info@viaduct.co.uk
• *Contemporary European
lighting*

Traditional

Ann's
34a–b Kensington
   Church Street
London W8 4HA
T: 020 7937 5033
* *Chandeliers. lamp bases
  and shades*

Bella Figura
G5 Chelsea Harbour
   Design Centre
Lots Road
London SW10 0XE
T: 020 7376 4564 *for stockists*
* *Classical and contemporary
  lighting*

Besselink & Jones
99 Walton Street
London SW3 2HH
T: 020 7584 0343
* *Wide range of lights*

Bhs plc
252–8 Oxford Street
London W1N 9DC
T: 020 7629 2011 *for branches*
* *Affordable traditional and
  modern fittings*

Charles Edwards
582 Kings Road
London SW6 2DY
T: 020 7736 8490
charles@charlesedwards.
   demon.co.uk
* *1780s onwards reproduction
  lights*

Christopher Hyde
180 Wandsworth Bridge Road
London SW6 2UF
T: 020 7731 8830
sales@christopherhyde.co.uk
* *Chandeliers, uplights, wall
  and table lamps*

Comet Lighting
43 Wolborough Street
Newton Abbott
Devon TQ12 1JG
T: 01626 332255
* *Brass wall, picture and desk
  lamps*

Hector Finch Lighting
88 Wandsworth Bridge Road
London SW6 2TF
T: 020 7731 8886
hector@hectorfinch.com
* *Antique lighting*

John Lewis Partnership
Oxford Street
London W1A 1EX
T: 020 7629 7711 *for branches*
JL_oxford_st@johnlewis.co.uk
* *Classic and contemporary
  styles*

Kensington Lighting
   Company
59 & 54a–b Kensington
   Church Street
London W8 4HA
T: 020 7938 2405
* *Traditional and modern
  lighting*

Liberty plc
Regent Street
London W1R 6AH
T: 020 7734 1234
* *Lighting Traditional and con-
  temporary*

McCloud Lighting
3rd floor, Unit 19–20
Chelsea Harbour Design
   Centre
London SW10 0XE
T: 020 7352 1533
sales@mccloud.co.uk
* *Hand-finished decorative
  lights*

Renwick & Clarke
190 Ebury Street
London SW1W 8UP
T: 020 7730 8913
* *Wood, metal and ceramic
  lights*

Tindle Lighting
162 Wandsworth Bridge Road
London SW6 2UQ
T: 020 7384 1485
* *Antique and decorative
  lighting*

Wilkinson plc
1 Grafton Street
London W1X 3LB
T: 020 7495 2477
* *Chandelier sales and repairs*

Christopher Wray
600 Kings Road
London SW6 2YW
T: 020 7736 8434 *for branches*
sales@christopherwray.com
* *Traditional lighting*

William Yeoward
Space S
The Old Imperial Laundry
71 Warriner Gardens
London SW11 4XW
T: 020 7498 4811
* *A selection of metal lamps*

Australia

De De Ce
263 Liverpool Street
Darlinghurst, NSW
T: 02 9360 2722
or
38 Little George Street
Fitzroy, Victoria
T: 03 9415 9599
dedece@bigpond.com

Euroluce
917 High Street
Armadale, Victoria
T: 03 9824 4611

Lightwise
99 Flinders Street
Darlinghurst, NSW
T: 02 9380 6222

New Zealand

ECC Lighting Ltd
39 Nugent Street
Grafton, Auckland
T: 09 379 9680

Lighting Direct
Auckland T: 09 529 1995
Christchurch T: 03 365 5370
Wellington T: 04 801 6125

Index

Figures in italics refer to captions

Author's acknowledgments

Many thanks to Sarah Roberts, Elaine Parker, Marie Claire Haselden and Christopher Fordham for all their invaluable help and advice.

Publisher's acknowledgments

The publisher would like to thank stylist Arabella McNie for her work on the dining table project on pages 44–5. Many thanks to all those who allowed their homes and gardens to be photographed. Thanks also to those who gave permission for their photographs to appear in this book: 1 VNU/Hans Zeegers/*Living;* 2 Ray Main/Mainstream; 5 Tom Stewart/lighting design by John Cullen Lighting; 6 Tom Stewart; 8 *World of Interiors*/Annabel Elston/lighting design David Gill; 9 above Undine Pröhl; 9 below Ray Main/Mainstream; 10 Lars Hallen/Design Press; 11 left Robert Harding Picture Library/James Merrell/© IPC Magazines Ltd/ *Homes & Gardens*/lighting design by John Cullen Lighting; 11 right Axiom/James Morris/architect Claudio Silvestrin; 12 above Ian McKinnell; 12 below View/Peter Cook/Woolf Architects; 14 Axiom/James Morris/lighting design by John Cullen Lighting/interior design by Lassman Interiors; 15 Axiom/James Morris; 16 Arcaid/ Richard Bryant/Paxton Locher Architects; 16-17 View/Chris Gascoigne/architect Norman Foster; 19 above left Ray Main/Mainstream/Yeoward; 19 above right Camera Press/*Schöner Wohnen;* 19 below David Spero/architect Seth Stein; 20 View/Chris Gascoigne/architect Seth Stein; 22 Axiom/James Morris/architect Will White; 23 Marianne Majerus; 24 Tom Stewart/lighting design by John Cullen Lighting/architecture and interior design by Oliver Morgan Architects; 25 above left & above right Tom Stewart; 25 above centre Tom Stewart/lighting design by John Cullen Lighting/interior design by Reed Creative; 25 below Ken Hayden/ interior design by Reed Creative; 26 left The Interior Archive/Fritz von der Schulenburg/architect Jean Oh; 26 right Ray Main/Mainstream/designer Llewelyn-Bowen; 27 Tim Street-Porter/Designer Brian Murphy; 28 left Tom Stewart/lighting design by John Cullen Lighting/architecture and interior design by Oliver Morgan Associates; 28 right Fritz von der Schulenburg/*House & Garden*/© The Condé Nast Publications Ltd/interior design by Lassman Interiors; 29 left Deidi von Schaewen; 29 right Ray Main/Mainstream; 30 Tom Stewart/lighting design by John Cullen Lighting/architecture and interior design by Oliver Morgan Architects; 31 left Tom Stewart/lighting design by John Cullen Lighting; 31 right Elizabeth Whiting & Associates/Michael Dunne; 32-33 Michael Moran/Moneo Brock Architects; 34-35 Ken Hayden/lighting design by John Cullen Lighting/ interior design by Reed Creative; 36-37 Tom Stewart/lighting design by John Cullen Lighting; 38-39 Richard Glover/architect John Pawson; 39 above Ray Main/Mainstream; 39 below Ray Main/Mainstream; 40 Ray Main/Mainstream; 41 *World of Interiors*/Henry Bourne; 42-43 Tom Stewart/lighting design by John Cullen Lighting; 44-45 Tom Stewart/lighting design by John Cullen Lighting/ architecture and interior design by Oliver Morgan Architects/Soft Furnishing by Reed Creative; 46-47 Tom Stewart/lighting design by John Cullen Lighting/ interior design by Lassman Interiors; 48 Axiom/James Morris; 49 Elizabeth Whiting & Associates; 50-51 Axiom/James Morris/lighting design by John Cullen Lighting/architecture and interior design by Littman Goddard Hogarth; 52 left Christophe Demonfaucon/architect François Roche; 52 right Ray Main/ Mainstream; 53 Axiom/James Morris/architect James Gorst; 54 above Axiom/ James Morris/architect Will White; 54 below Tom Stewart/lighting design by John Cullen Lighting/interior Design by Reed Creative; 55 left Ken Hayden/ lighting design by John Cullen Lighting/interior design by Reed Creative; 55 right View/Dennis Gilbert; 56-57 Axiom/James Morris/lighting design by John Cullen Lighting/interior design by Tim Boyd and Alex Michaelis Associates; 57 Tom Stewart/lighting design by John Cullen Lighting/interior design by Tim Boyd and Alex Michaelis Associates; 58 View/Chris Gascoigne/architect Seth Stein; 59 Axiom/James Morris; 60-61 The Interior Archive/Fritz von der Schulenburg/lighting design by John Cullen Lighting/interior design Todhunter Earle; 62 Axiom/James Morris/architect John Pawson; 63 *World of Interiors*/ Annabel Elston; 64 Axiom/James Morris/architect John Pardey; 65 above © One Aldwych, London/lighting design by Lighting Design International/interior design by Mary Fox Linton; 65 below Ray Main/Mainstream designer Spencer Fung; 66 View/Dennis Gilbert/architect Rick Mather; 67 View/ Chris Gascoigne; 68 left Ray Main/Mainstream; 68 right View/Dennis Gilbert/ architect Bernhard Blauel; 69 Ken Hayden/lighting design by John Cullen Lighting/interior design by Reed Creative; 70 Paul Ryan/International Interiors/ architects Pierce & Allen; 71 Axiom/James Morris; 72 Arcaid/Earl Carter/ Belle/architect Grey Anderson; 73 Tom Stewart; 74-75 Ken Hayden/interior design by Reed Creative; 76 *Marie Claire Maison*/Gilles de Chabaneix/ Catherine Ardouin; 77 left Ray Main/Mainstream; 77 right *Marie Claire Maison*/Nicolas Tosni/J Borgeaud; 78 Christian Sarramon; 79 Marianne Majerus/lighting effect designed by George Carter; 80 View/Peter Cook; 80-81 Axiom/James Morris/lighting design by John Cullen Lighting/garden design by R K Alliston; 81 Marianne Majerus/lighting effect designed by George Carter; 82-83 Tom Stewart/lighting design by John Cullen Lighting/garden design by Arne Maynard; 84 Camera Press/*Schöner Wohnen;* 85 Tom Stewart/ lighting design by John Cullen Lighting/Garden Design by Arne Maynard; 86 Ray Main/ Mainstream; 89 Axiom/James Morris; 91 Tom Stewart; 92-97 Patrick McLeavy; 99 Tom Stewart.